MALEANTE
Blackbird Toledo

Maleante

© 2019 by Blackbird Toledo

ISBN (Softcover): 978-1-54398-950-2
ISBN (eBook): 978-1-54398-951-9

Contents

Chapter 1

icture this: A NYC ghetto kid bamboozled, swindled out of her life. Well, money in the bank, a couple grand in the first drawer, finishing up my bachelor's degree. Got a three-bedroom condo, with a nice car. So, how? According to my professor, with my factors, 99.9% chance I won't make it. I laughed when she said that. "I'm in control of my own life of course." I thought to myself. I'm about to see how right she is.

Mom wakes up in the hospital after having me. The woman in the room nearby says to her, "Look, my baby's really hungry." When my mom looked, it was me in someone else's arms. Almost switched at birth.

POW! I see Little Eric fly through the air, a hit-and-run on our way to school. He lived though. Headed to the cuchifritos spot, BOOM! Someone shot at us three little girls in the car. The bullet missed me and hit the head of my seat. I was playing on the floor of the car... While me and cousin walk home one day...BAM!

"Why you punch him in the face?" "Run your Chinese shoes." "Okay."

"Mommy, please don't drink no more." It was Christmas Eve. I dragged her in the house that day all peed up. I couldn't carry her; she was too heavy. I put a pillow under her head so she could sleep. She was tired.

School was no different. Gladys was the bitch in 1st grade that started me off. She grabbed my pickle, put her nail in it and told me, "I want half." I've been fighting ever since to get and keep a meal.

Growing up in the hood, burnt buildings are our jungle gyms. The back alleys were a secret world filled with kids, connected with the fire escapes. People used them like patios, for hanging laundry, or growing plants. Other kids would do all kinds of flips and stunts on them, but I was careful. I thought it would break off or come loose and it did. It didn't break off completely, just hanging off the building for a year. The whole block saw when it happened. Too much jumping on it, I guess.

One night, I'm walking to the bodega with my mom. The 4 train rolls by. I see crazy eyes. My grip on my mom's hand tightened as we crossed the street. All of a sudden, he grabs me and starts pulling on my legs mid-air. I'm yelling and screaming as he's trying to pull me into the park. That's when the bodega man comes out. I'm thinking he'll help us. He looks out, and locks the store, leaving me and Mom to fight. Just then, the twins who lived on the floor under, came out and chased him away with a bat.

My mom did hair for extra money sometimes. One day while she is doing Titi's hair, she steps out to get some hair spray. My aunt's boyfriend rings the doorbell and we open to see he's got a hole in his neck. "Mommy, where are you?" I didn't see her. I find out later the shooter ran past my mom. We knew if you looked, you die. Fortunately, we didn't look. Cops never asked and we never told. The rules were set.

At the beach, Mom took me out all the way to the buoys in the ocean. Then, she told me to swim back and swam away. I remembered "Booty up" and floated back to shore. I was so scared it felt like I was having a heart attack. A lot of my childhood was spent in ERs for everything from lung collapses to pneumonia. I didn't let anyone know; it would be considered weakness.

I'm 10 now, and I got my first job volunteering at the nursing home. I played bingo and read the newspaper with the elderly there. I met Fannie. She was so wise, and she told me that I was worth it. I came to work the next day and she was gone. She went to heaven.

A house full of alcoholics. Crack had just come out and all my friends' parents seemed to be on it. My best friend Mel was getting hurt. She'd show me the bruises on her legs. It wasn't from normal beatings. I felt lucky to just get whipped. There were many kids like Mel, and Jade, and Jo, and Michi, and Lisa. I would ask her, "Who's doing that to you?" and she'd say, "He'll kill my family." No one talked about the kids who got hurt; they just protected the bad guys.

Mom put me in a program called Fresh Air Fund in Harlem; they take poor kids to nice places. Truddi was nice. She lived the opposite of the Bronx at her house. We ate vegetables and swam in her pond. I went to Vermont for a couple of summers to visit and it was wonderful. Me and my friend from there, Monique, went out to swim one time, when kids started pointing at us. I said, "They wanna swim with us." Monique said, "No." Then I heard them say, "Look, niggers!" We held each other, and we cried.

Mom sent me and baby Krissy to the corner store. Krissy got ran over by a car. She lived though.

Vicky (Mom's other side), told me I had to rob the Bolita man (number man) Jose. I did not want to. Being a little kid and you're in a strange house, what do I take? I took the microwave; I figured we didn't have one. When I got upstairs, she said, "Put that shit back." I had to climb down the fire escape and put it back. She reminded me, "Don't forget he has a gun."

When I was very young, Vicky took me out and dressed me up beautiful one day. New coat, new shoes. Everything was good... until we got arrested.

At the time when the other girls were getting their hair done in curls, I asked my mom to get my first haircut. We went to the shop and I was excited. I stared in the mirror. The happiness was short-lived and drained out of me when I saw a red, white, and blue sign (Barbershop). Then a man put clippers to the back of my head. I quickly realized I wasn't in a beauty shop. Vicky had my head shaved. One tear rolled down my check because Vicky didn't allow me to cry...

I always knew when she'd come back. Sis asked me how you know. I just did. She's scary, she tortures you, and she'll take your self-esteem. Shame is her specialty. Chairs, brooms, belts, shoes: she'll hit with whatever's next to her and her mouth never closes. I had to lie to the doctor when she broke my hand. I remember thinking, "I'll never lie for you again."

She invited us to her therapy place when she started getting rehab...once. When I started to talk, she said, "You promised not to tell!" and ran off.

Just like that she's back to normal, combing your hair, cleaning your room, making you food. "Mom, they threw tear gas at us today." "Too bad.", she replies. "Mom they robbed me; I lost everything." She says, "Oh, I had a bad day."

These streets will turn a church kid into a stick-up kid. On the train going to school, I see the guy who sells batteries get smacked up and robbed. No one did anything about it. It was just like that. I felt sorry for the guy.

My grandma sent us out, so we were playing at the Jonny pump (fire hydrant). Kids everywhere, and music blasting. When the streets turned to blood. A kid got hit by a car. I cried for days, my mom told me. Cars were wild back then, no rules, people going a hundred miles per hour on the side street. They announced during school that a classmate playing chicken on the back of a bus did not survive. Tommy, my best friend and next-door neighbor growing up, got ahold of his father's gun and shot himself. Not long after, his father died of a broken heart.

One day, Pops gave me a set of clippers and told me rob the store he works at. I soon realized they didn't cut, so I looked around the back and found a box of Snapple. I didn't want to come home empty-handed.

Chapter 2

ev dropped a 9mm in the middle of science class. "But I thought we had metal detectors," I said to myself. It was different from going to Catholic school. Evander Childs was filled with a bunch of misguided and neglected kids. Nothing like the spoiled brats in Catholic school who had everything. Here it was okay to be poor. The Church gave me a great education and it had a beautiful library though.

While waiting for the bus with Ito, a kid I grew up with, they jump out on us. He had half a bag of weed on him. They start to pummel him. Circling him and kicking. I heard him quietly say, "It's just a little bit."

I saw my classmate Richard break a 40-ounce beer in Sundance's face. Just as soon as he bought it, coming out the store, he used it. SMASH. I didn't feel bad because Sundance had punched me in the breast when I would not go out with his friend. It formed a lump and I had to get surgery to remove it.

At the end of the school year, I decided I was done with it. I dropped out, and enrolled myself in John Jay college, after taking my GED. 16 years old and somehow, I was asked to join and ended up on the basketball team playing full court games. It was hard, but I just played aggressive and throwing elbows at people. They loved me. I was a college basketball player by accident.

One summer I bumped into some friends of mine at Orchard Beach. They were riding motorcycles. One of the guys asked me to get on a motorcycle with him, and we crashed. I jumped off before it spun out. He got peeled up pretty bad. His name is Santien. Later on, he invited me to come to his block. It's really tough over there. His best friend, Polo hung Cookout by his feet, off a rooftop for trying to snitch on Santien. Every Thursday, kids get swept up and aren't seen till Monday at the courts. One time, I see what I think is a homeless man on the ground groaning. He rolled over and I saw he was shot. I picked up the pay phone to call 911. They never came and I didn't wait for them.

On my way to school, I get stop and frisked. I tried to explain that I was a John Jay student. His reply was, "That's just in movies." I say, "But, I'm studying about kids in poor communities." They bring me to the precinct. They said I fit the description of someone they were looking for. I said, "It wasn't me", and they let me go. Mothers, daughters, sisters are the ones left suffering. Some women are just getting catfished, working to fill up commissaries. 10/10 never stay with the girl. If I cry, I'll be dead next. I hate weakness.

I remember watching Flaco doing his signature move, climbing on to his victim's back, putting his knee on their spine, and choke-holding them until they went down in a few seconds. When they woke up, they realized their pockets were inside out. Sometimes, they were so drunk or high that they wouldn't know what happened. He got so good at robbing, he robbed stores from the rooftops.

At the first block party I went to, music was plugged in by a streetlamp. While listening to KRS, shots rang out. I get down like everyone else. People are frozen, waiting, when the shooting stops. The gunman runs right by me and people start running again. I tripped over something; that's when I saw him, open eyed and laid out. I jumped over him. He was gone. No police or EMT. Just kids crowding. I asked God to forgive me for stepping over him.

A good friend of mine had a baby. It was a surprise because we didn't even know she was pregnant. She told me, she had the baby in the bathtub because if her grandma found out, she'd be homeless. She ended up homeless. I told her to come to my job to get clothes for the baby. I got caught and had to pay the money back. I got a new job at a deli and she got her first apartment through a program called Section

8. You could only get ghetto apartments. She started to let drug dealers use her apartment as a stash house. One night, I didn't go to work, and the next day everyone tells me Biggie showed up. He got a sandwich, some philly cigars, and left a 100-dollar bill.

We were looking out the window on a cold night, when the paddy wagons roll up. They sweep up the whole block. "Now's our chance," she said. "Huh?" She starts stuffing the drugs in a book bag. Then she says to me, "Grab the guns." I took two small handguns and a Tec-9. I put the two in my front pockets and the Tec on my waist. I thought it was like the movies, where it magically stays on your waist. By the time we got down the fire escape, it fell down my pants. Good thing I tucked my socks over my jeans; the gun stayed in my jeans and Timberlands. Also, it keeps the jeans' dye off the kicks.

The next day I see Flaco. He tries out the handguns in his closet. When I peeked in the closet, there were bullet holes all over. I said to him, "Won't it ricochet?" He says, "It's the projects."

I sell them to a friend for 300 dollars and I kept the Tec-9. I start to hear different voices coming from my gun saying, "Aren't I pretty? Touch me, you know I work." I thought about the man who robbed me on the subway. He grabbed my friend and I said, "Let her go!" So, then he grabs me instead. He snatched my chain so hard; I nearly fell in the tracks while she ran and left me. Mom said, "Good for your ass."

In the morning, I catch the iron horse (train) to work, then back to night school, and home. It's madness there. I barely sleep. My parents fighting, I can't take it. Pops hit me with a crowbar in the head so hard, the scar is still there... My baby sisters with no guidance. I did my best to take care of them. Neighborhood riots every day because nobody had jobs, too busy selling drugs and doing witchcraft.

The voices would say to me, "You could get that money real quick."

Something was changing inside of me. I lacked any emotions except for anger. So, I decided to try it, my first stickup. I picked someone who I thought wouldn't fight back and looked weak. They call it a "sweet victim" or "sweet vick" for short. He fought me for my gun, and we wrestled all over Jerome Avenue. I had my finger blocking the trigger the whole time thinking, "He's going to shoot me with my own gun." Finally, he let go and I ran to the roof of the nearest building to stash my gun. That was not for me.

I was still in law school at the time, thinking of other ways to get paid. Stupid career thing was taking too long. Four or five more years of school to get some dough.

"How will I make it?" "I won't, that's how."

I decided to get rich selling drugs. I got my own stamp and bought my own stuff with some money I saved. My aunt who was a known heroin addict was going to help me get rid of it. She got rid of it alright. She used it all. This really stinks. I can't hurt someone for ten dollars.

The guys are getting paid now. Junkies sleepwalking all over NYC. They were like zombies. When I took my crew to Bloomingdales for the first time, they went wild. It was cool to watch them run through the men's department, in competition, grabbing everything. The price didn't matter, only the size: Large and extra-large. One day in a music video, I saw gold fronts and I wanted them. I got tops and bottoms. When I hung out with the guys, that whole night I never said a word. Me and Merc caught the munchies and were eating pickles. The guys noticed and went crazy. The next day at least four of my friends got them. You know the saying "shop till you drop?" I did it once, I bought so much junk, I couldn't make it fit in the Acura Legend. My arms held those leather jackets like a walking rack. I kept doing crazy shopping sprees until I had filled up my whole room with sweaters, hoodies, jeans, jackets, leathers, sneakers, boots. Santien tried to outdo me. I found out he had a crackhead steal him the whole Tommy summer rugby collection. The rolling racks and all. Cars, we collect them, get bored, and throw it out. Leave it at a bus stop. As long as you take your plates off, you good.

Don't get me started on the cars cause there's only one thing that comes to mind: New Jersey. My friends in Jersey were amazing to watch. It's like second nature; they jump up out of the rocks and steal the whole block's cars.

Not the foreign ones though. Beaver said, "Those are too hard." Stealing cars was how they were able to get around and come to the boroughs. My boy asked me to drive him home because he wasn't feeling well. "I never drove stick shift before," I said. He says, "I don't care. It ain't mine."

My friend of affluence, her parents owned a fruit market or two, would have to give in her tuition, and she would not give it to Sister Patricia to steal it. That turned into her robbing the register when her parents would not give her money. Which, in a short time, turned to her calling the Burnside boys to stick her own store up. When I saw the old lady with tape on her glasses because they punched her in the face, I became afraid of spoiled brats who can so easily turn on their family. She said that she wanted them to beat her father up because he cheated on her mom. Your own blood?

Chapter 3

 dropped myself off at the club and had a blast. Palladium, Rose Land, Club 2000, Fever, or Jimmy's Cafe, to name a few stomping grounds. We never waited on lines; you just give the bouncer 100 bucks. Famous rappers and big dogs would send us bottles, trying to get our attention. We wouldn't even open them. It was fun coming from nothing.

Prodigy loves my block; he came to the Puerto Rican Day parade with us once. We had a cooler of Hennessy and it spilled out by mistake. Out comes the plastic Glock. The cops were right there and pretended not to notice. He stayed with us the whole time. Maybe he felt he could let his guard down a little.

Street fights were every few minutes... A mob of chicks talking, blah blah, starts heading my way. I'm thinking, "They're coming for me?" One girl comes and swings at me. She misses and I hit her over the head with a pay phone. CLONK CLONK. The noise scared me. I had to stop myself from breaking the phone on her head and I ran.

At a house party, a girl scratched a DJ's record and all hell breaks loose. Next thing you know, one of the small dunnies got swept up and tumbled by the mob. A guy with a hammer starts swinging and I got knocked out.

A friend of mine got stabbed at a house party. Later on, his father went to court with a gun and shot the guy at trial for vengeance. The judge said he was legally insane.

People avoided violence entirely by staying inside. We didn't have that luxury. My mom says, "Get out." Every morning. Some people paid the price for staying in all day: They became hoarders or obese.

Don't play hip-hop music near the NYPD. I learned it the hard way. I'm driving home from work, one night, and I got pulled over. They pull up guns drawn on me, threw me on my face crucifix-style, nose-down on the ground. After they searched me and didn't find anything, they say, "These are yours." to a Ziploc full of bullets. I say, "No they're not." So, they threw my Bo Jackson sneakers over the fence...

Chapter 4

That's when I heard his voice for the first time. I look up, I see a grim reaper black hoodie. "Ya'll mothafuckas work for me now!" A neck full of gold, .40 caliber in hand, and a big pair of black Timberlands. He starts lining up workers, emptying their pockets for whatever junk dope they were selling. He took his burner out and clapped Kid, one of the well-known small fries, in the face. Not to kill him but to shake the block, and the whole block shivered. Everyone sells Bodega now. He had a "10/10," according to the junkies. Whatever it was, they went nuts. The next day, everyone had switched sides. The message echoed loud and clear: there's a new King on the block and in his own words, "Anyone selling something else is leaving in a body bag."

Guys who I respected were now hard to look at the same. So-called "tough guys" weren't so tough anymore. Once a man honked his horn at him. King, without saying a word, walked over to his trunk, pulled out a bat, and busted out the guy's windows. One side at a time. Windshield, passenger side, then the driver's window. I'm sure that man never used his horn again.

At a club, he seen a worker of his who robbed some bundles (work) and ran away. He was dancing and popping champagne, forgetting he robbed the wrong person. He got punched in the face so hard with the left, that he fell asleep. I saw a knot growing on his head as security dragged him by the arms and legs and threw him out the club. King snatched his necklace and said, "Pay what you owe!"

He's a force and he cleaned that block up quickly. No more robbing drug dealers, no one robbing old people, and the money was in the hundreds of thousands.

A Mac-10 and a jammed gun. An assassination attempt failed. King dragged the man down at least 2 blocks while he was hanging off the side of the car.

In the middle of Manhattan, he starts saying, "I ran out of money." and told me to drive. He gets out and goes into a store. Next thing you know, he's running toward me with a bag of money. I said, "What'd you do?" He said, "They owed me."

Poor, rich, I seen 'em all copping dope. It wasn't long before my girls were doing it. When I was throwing up one night from too much drinking, I heard the girls coming in the bathroom. I was too beat-up to make myself seen, but then I heard it: Sniff sniff. After that one of my homegirls got caught at the airport with her baby for smuggling drugs.

NYPD pull us over one day. They snatched up King and put him in a car. I thought he was kidnapped because I called the precinct, and no one heard from him. A few hours later I hear the music coming down the block, and a beat up and robbed King calls me out. I run down and he spins me in the air. I can't believe it; they let him go. He said, "They just wanted money." We got an apartment and we filled it with treasures of all kinds. Crackheads sell you everything: gold, diamonds; I even saw someone sell a fan once.

I just kept wondering, was my professor, right? Was this sociological perspective thing going to get me? Does it have me already? I heard a man say he was afraid for his baby to be born because life around here was only worth five bucks.

Chapter 5

ing grew up in Spofford. He got that name for being only 13 in jail. He got out and went back in until he was 18. His family dynamic changed when he got home. His 12-year-old sister was now a mother, his mother was selling drugs, and he was thrown back in the mix. In one month, he was already counting half a million dollars in the hallway while I would look

out for cops and repeat. He took over and ran a few blocks besides ours. At re-up time I asked King,

"Who could ever think a little old man like that could feed the whole city dope?"

One day he had a rapper washing his car when his song came on the radio. I looked down and there he was, washing King's rims. Rappers were under us?

A man hit me in front of him. So, he shot as his feet and made him run so fast.

Another time we go horseback riding. We got on with our group, and he tells the horse something in its ear. His horse speeds off and mine after them, running down the Bronx River. I was terrified. The horses kept eating the leaves off the trees while cars on the freeway honked at us. We ended up at the beach. A few hours later, we found our guide and ran away laughing.

One of the thotties from the block got pregnant by a married man around this time. She was having a baby shower, and she kept telling me to go. The car made strange sounds that night on the way and decides to go clunk in the middle of the street. While we waited for a tow truck, my feet swinging out the window, he said, "Give me a kiss." I did. I thought I saw a shadow beside me, so I looked again, and I saw it, a gunman walking to the side of our car. Then the sounds started. I hear them flying by me. He swings open the door, hitting the guy. They start fighting and I hear him say, "Watch out, Ma!" I run the opposite way of where they're wrestling. I hear the shots still. I take another glance in the corner of my eye, and I see another one. He has a bigger gun.

My legs are noodles and I see fire, BOOM, BOOM! I cover my ears; I see him running and the floor is full of shells. The smell of gunpowder fills my nose, then I look to the floor to check for blood. None. I start to run towards where he is when a cop grabs my arm. I scream, "Where is he?!" He says, "They took him to the hospital, he's going to be fine." "Get in the car." I said I have to check on him. He walkie-talked his partner and they confirmed he was stable and at the hospital. I went with them. When I got to the precinct, I could hear them say, "They shot the King of Bodega."

The interrogation began and I told them everything I saw. They got angry, pulling out a book, saying, "Who's this? Who's that?" They had masks and hoodies. "Who did it?" "I don't know." I say, "I didn't see their faces."

"Get her out of here! He's dead anyway." I tried to walk. I couldn't so I fell down the precinct stairs. I heard a cop say, "Do you know who the fuck they just killed?" It can't be, he was just fighting the guy. Is this a dream? I'm not processing what just happened. I remember thinking about the war that would happen. Would they blow up the whole spot?

I go straight to his mother and she says, "Why are you alive?"

At that time, my cousin got killed by vehicular homicide. It was horrible. My grandma came upstairs, barely able to stand, yelling "Mataron a Nicky!" We found out that he was riding with his friends to the store and the driver crashed.

One way or another the streets were taking everyone.

Chapter 6

heard the name of the people who robbed me. It was time to get them. I took two of my boys. Powers was shaking and twitching. He had a taser. I said, "Chill." I turn to look at my friend O and he's got the eyes. He had just got home from doing eight years, not even a month ago. He told me a story of how blood makes noise when it leaks. I asked, "How?". He said when it pumps out it makes a sound; he gave somebody a buck fifty

on the face. Maybe I reminded myself of that story so we could be ready to do what we were about to do.

I knock on the door and the snake answered. I walked in looking around for anything that belongs to me. I ask, "Who's here?" No one. Just then, I hear someone in the bathroom. "You lied." "You said no one was here." "My boys about to lay you down here." I peeped my homeboy; his eyes were dilated. It wasn't right to ask him to do this. It was selfish. My boy was going to do another bid, for me? When no one else cares? I had a split-second decision to shoot or walk away, and I walked away. A few days after that, I saw the SWAT team raid their house. Turns out, they were climbing in people's windows and robbing. I didn't have to use the .357 Dirty Harry after all.

My boy Flaco invites us girls out to eat. We all get in the car and make a stop at the Buddha spot. He asked them for ten bags and starts to drive away. The Jamaicans start cussing, screaming, "BUMBACLOT!" "PUSSYCLOT MON!" and lock off the front and back exits. They punch him in the face, drag him out the window, and step on his face. He keeps saying sorry, but they keep clobbering him. Us girls roll out, flying down the killer stairs five at a time, knowing if you miss a step, you die. Those stairs are legend in the Bronx. We make it to Jerome Ave, and I ask his girl, "Don't you care?" She's outta there. Then we hear the shots. When we get back to the block, we tell the guys what happened. They don't even budge, acting as if nothing happened. I was sad for him, but he shows up, out of the moonlight, completely swelled shut eyes, and knotted up. Instant karma. He robbed the wrong ones. Good thing they spared his life.

Chapter 7

e and Santien went to the premier of *Godfather III*. When we were leaving the Loew's Paradise movie theater, we see the cops having a shootout with this guy named Trouble. Boy did they shoot. It looked like a Wild West movie. Maybe it was the movie, maybe it was the full moon, but there were brains all over the street that night. May he rest in peace.

I'm now pregnant with the young man I told you about at Orchard Beach on the motorcycles. Yeah, he's my baby father. At the baby's doctor's appointment, the doc says I have toxemia. "Okay, what's that?" "It means you have to have the baby today." Santien had court that day as usual. I think to myself, "He always gets postponed." When the hospital phone starts to ring, it's his best friend Polo and he tells me Santien was remanded. I drop the phone and look down. My water broke. I did not want to have my baby all alone.

Of course, I did.

So began the year of Rikers Island.

"You ain't gotta be in jail to do time." I'm on the other side, the visitors' side, and on one occasion I was told, "Step aside." When I did, the C.O. puts up a yellow barrier between me and the others, then tells me, "Pull your pants down." I said, "No." She says, "Now." I reluctantly did it then she screams, "Panties too!" I almost cried, then she told me to squat. Never had I been so humiliated. When she sees I'm hiding nothing, she tells me throw away my calculator. It was contraband. On some occasions, his mom would sneak weed in balloons. The picture guy would retrieve it from the garbage and give it to Santien. He'll call me so happy. I started hearing rumors on the block about how he ran the sprungs (jail houses) and C76. When he came home, it was out of control. He made so many connections in jail.

Between lawyers and bail there was no money left, right? I put my daughter to sleep with her dad and start getting ready to head out to work when out the window I hear the guys screaming, "Pussy whipped!" He always got ridiculed for having a girlfriend. I reminded him that I had to go to work and he tells me, "The shit is real." We tussle. I knock over a picture and behind it was a hole in the wall. When I look, I see tens of thousands of dollars. I mean big BRICKS. Cruel irony. When I'm working every day. I walk out, leaving him with the baby, never thinking he left his baby.

The next morning, I call him on my break to check on my baby, when I see my boss eyeballing me. I was late that morning because of a huge accident on the highway. When they finally answer the phone, it was my sister. I ask,

"Why are you answering the phone?!". I hear screaming and wailing. "Where's my baby!?" "What happened?!"

"Santien, he's dead."

The next few days were very blurry. With no life, no dreams, and no plans. At his wake people partied, drank, and even went home together. I brought my gun to the funeral because you never know what is going to happen. The hood don't love nobody. It recruits new players daily, characters change, and in one week a new operation was already in play. They took him back to Puerto Rico to be buried and I never saw him again.

At that time, Polo was there for my baby. He brought her pajamas, toys, and gifts. We mourned by smoking weed. That day was like the rest. My beeper went off, and Polo says, "Let's chill." That night we go to Blackbox on 122nd and then to eat. We had chilled so many times throughout the years, but I never noticed how beautiful he was. I knew the girls went crazy over him. He puts his arm around me, playing Tupac "How do you want it?" and brings me close to him. My heart skips then, BAM, out of nowhere we crash. He calls me a witch, we laugh, we kissed good night, and I'm a princess. I got his beep the next morning, "See you tonight." We made plans and I wondered what I would wear. I go outside to the bodega and I see people screaming at me. I heard the Diaz brother say, "They killed your man." I grabbed him by his collar, "What you said?" "Watch your fucking mouth." Then I heard the streets whisper, "He's dead."

Chapter 8

The burning buildings, the chickens running by. I can't take it anymore. Living in the darkest corners of the South Bronx, where taxis don't stop. Believe me, I had to point my gat at one's face to get him to stop. Some people were following me, I thought they were going to try to rob me. I waved the heat to scare them off. They were scared... until they saw the revolver chamber was empty. One of 'em yelled, "She ain't got no bullets!"

After he let me in, I apologized. He said, "No problem."

They found Little Jayshon in a bathtub. He was trying to get away from the fire spreading. He was only a kid... They had a little truck and bike of his at the memorial. The whole neighborhood was devastated. The numerous fires in our run-down buildings claimed so many lives. A lot were started by the building owners to get an insurance payday. Afterwards, our pit bull wouldn't walk near there. She would howl and cry, something she never done.

Someone got kidnapped; it was on the news. They found him in the basement, burnt and chopped up. Perro, a guy from the block, got shot twelve times and lived. Liza, a little girl nearby, got hit with a stray in the shoulder and did not.

When I saw Gee put back Half-Pint's intestines, I had a new idea. I could be a doctor and sew people up to save lives. My grandmother once told me, "If you take a life, you lose yours." So, what happens when you save one?

Chapter 9

am thankful to be alive and keep trying to start over when forbidden love hits, my knight in shining armor. I thought he was perfect, the guy downstairs. Everyone told me Method Man was downstairs. When I went down, we locked eyes and were inseparable. He was the most handsome thing I'd ever seen. They called him "Jordan of the streets", whenever he plays ball, it would gather crowds of people. That kid was talented. He could

even dunk with a baby on his back. He could've gone to the NBA. After a couple of karate movies and Chinese food, we are pregnant.

We are getting sandwiches in the middle of the night, when a Lincoln Continental pulls up. I see two guys laid in the back, and one in the front with his seat leaned back. He jumps out to grab me, so I run in the store. I head to the back of the store; I knew they gambled there. I grabbed a nearby phone to call Awol. I wasn't sure if he'd come, so I plan my escape. Looking through the glass windows, I see him with an AR-15 in his hands like a beast. That thing was huge. We played the walls, walking zigzag until we got to a neighboring building, then jumped the rooftops to safety.

I lost my job when my boss noticed I had a bump. He works at Hunts Point but it's hardly enough. His mother asked, "I wonder what color they'll be?". I thought, "What a strange question." "Brown and Brown go just fine." "We both were neighbors my whole life." I went to school, ate, and played with all people. I thought a person's status depends on salary. He doesn't come home that night and I wonder,

"Where is he?" I call him, no answer. I see his mom and she says to me, "Oh, he had to go do some jail time."

Left alone again, my doctor schedules a C-section. I say, "No." They tie me up with straps and tell me, "Don't push." I push anyway. The doctors start yelling at me to "Stop pushing!" I said, "I can't." 1 Baby A, BOOM, then 2 Baby B. All the doctors said, "Breech delivery didn't exist anymore." The nurse then whispered in my ear, "You're good." That night I stared at the sky. I couldn't believe what just happened: Four arms, four legs. Twins.

He comes home from jail and we have another baby, she's the most beautiful sight I ever laid eyes on. People would come up to stare at her. I'm finishing my medical degree, new apartment, new car—what could go wrong? Well, his little bro got sentenced to twenty years. He started wearing red every day after that. He wore it for his brother because he took the blame for something, they both did.

One night hanging at the pool room, my boy Merc was wearing all blue when 4 or 5 guys pull up. They start surrounding us screaming, "BLLATT" "BLLATT" to hype themselves up. "Is that Merc over there?", they say. They start to pound on him. He shells up and tries to run out. I get in my car and start driving. I see him waving at me yelling and I pick him up. Sometimes you got to catch a beat down. I wondered why he did not fight back. All the sadness must take the fight out of you.

Awol wore this red Pelle leather a lot, so I sliced it with a box cutter. All this color stuff was taking lives. He didn't come home that night. One day turned to a week, then I'd see him once a month. I always thought he was dead; his mother always assured me he was alive. I had a plan this time to get out! I saved a few G's and got a condo. Life is alright. Yes, I waited for my Awol to come through the school doors and say, "I love my babies," but he never did.

Chapter 10

beauty like that... "Why?" is what I asked her. I was confused. There was a person waiting for her in a hotel. I did not want to take her, but I didn't want her to go alone. Against my third eye, I start taking her. The hood of my car flies open as we are on the highway and she tries to run out. "My trick is waitin'. I'll take a taxi." I say, "No." and close it. I drop her off and she tells me to wait. Fighting tears and the overwhelming feeling

to drive away, I stay, 15 minutes later she gets back in the car never looking up once. So pretty. One of the most beautiful I've seen. She's got short black hair, big black eyes, and red lips. I dropped her back to Hunts Point, where she said. A few weeks pass by, and I ask Divine, "Where'd she go?" He tells me, "You didn't hear?" "They found her body in the Hudson River."

"Why was she doing that?" I yelled at him. He said, "She was always E'd up." I guess that meant pills.

I go out one night with my girls and that's all I remember. I woke up in a strange room with my pants down. I touched myself—what's wrong? I ran home and took baths for days. I was afraid to go to the hospital because I was scared. "Am I dying?" I wondered for a while. I finally had the nerve to take the tests. Everything was ok.

There was something at that time called OJ's. It's renting a taxi by the hour. You could do crimes, smoke weed, and play really loud music. Our OJ honked at the Old Dirty Bastard and he flew out his car screaming at the top of his lungs, beating our driver. We giggled. The driver became one of our regulars and stayed with us in the clubs. His name's 43. A fight broke out and some guys were flying around. Literally, I see a guy get tossed like a frisbee. 43 pulls out his badge to get us out of there, saying he's a cop. Oh shit, I done seen it all. He was an undercover? 43 has seen so much with us, we had him for two years and he always has had our back. He took me to the cemetery once, to visit un amigo, and he asked me to promise to put a flower on his grave if he died.

One day, my little sister tells me, "I'm leaving to the Marines in the morning." Just like that. I didn't get a chance to talk her out of it. Must've been all our veteran blood.

Cops are not so bad after all. Both my sisters married one. Who else do you call when you're shot and bleeding, 911.

Chapter 11

'm getting older and my clock is ticking. But my paranoia won't allow me to trust anyone. Loud noises gave me mini heart attacks. My boy always said, "If you're scared, get a dog." That is exactly what we did. A Pitbull. After grandma had shot up the living room, we decided no more guns. No one got hurt though.

Somewhere along the chaos, me and Mom bonded. I fell in love with her, I adore her, and I am forever in her debt. Vicky stays on vacation most of the time.

Dad and I went fishing a lot, it helped me conquer fear of water. The calm sounds of the ocean, the fact that I wasn't afraid of worms, or maybe even the time I caught a shark with him. I don't know what about that fishing, but I formed the greatest respect for dad. Pop came to NYC from Puerto Rico with his big family. He did everything to help his mom and siblings. Starting off shining shoes at 8 years old. His father cut sugar cane to make a living and to send the kids to the United States for schools. Grandpa found work in a belt making factory. Abuela, on the other hand, had it hard coming from Cuba. Her mom died in her arms, of Tuberculosis. Thankfully her mother gave birth to her in Florida, which made Abuela a U.S citizen.

Pops was working at Dean Witter in the World Trade Center at the time, when Mom did domestic violence and scratched him in the face. He didn't go to work that day.

At my job, happy computer/phone people. It's almost like no one knows what happened here. I thought about a house, a fence. Against my better judgment's warning, a fellow co-worker asked me out on a date. He started to pop up at my places and I considered it an act of kindness or flattery. He liked music, cars, fishing, and cooking just like me. But he was a con artist, a shapeshifter. He didn't like my mother, sister, or my kids. Eventually... wait, I'm getting ahead. It started when he pretended to do everything I did. He had no children, so when I found out I was pregnant, that was just what we needed. Our family marveled at the sweet joy. Sadly, we were mistaken; his baby turned into "Give me MY baby."

While I was pregnant the abuse began. He threw me down a flight of stairs and said he tripped. He broke my arm and said it was a mistake, sorry. The abuse was confusing. After an attack he would start crying and saying he wants his baby. I tried to explain that he didn't want the baby, acting so violent and he slapped me in the face while I breastfed my son. I heard my ancestors say, "The yets, have yet to come."

Then he was gone. No stalking, no breaking phones, no accusations, just peace… and just like that, he's literally punching down my door. I call the cops, but they don't come. The next morning, I find him in front of my door sleeping. He's everywhere: my job, the supermarket, the kids' school, the window, even the garbage disposal. He jumps out from behind a tree. He punches me in the mouth, and I spit teeth. I punch him so hard his nose moves over. We fight head-to-head at this point; he's trying to kill me. His punches feel scary. I remember my mother's voice telling me, "If you kill him in your house, it's okay." I hear a different voice say, "Jala gatillo" (Pull the trigger). Mommy, I don't want to go to hell.

I wondered what to do; I'm running out of options. Everything I had escaped in childhood. I call a place called Horizon and they sit me with a child who looks younger than my kids, asking me how I feel. Who the fuck cares how I feel? I need help.

It's my son's birthday. I'm returning with bags and cake then I hear it: the most disgusting voice. He's back. He runs in my house. I start to tell him, it's ok, I'll let him see the baby, when he grabs a staple gun from my kitchen and starts stapling his face and punching his face at the same time. There's blood pouring off his face. I told him the grocery delivery was downstairs as a lure and he switches back like nothing, wiping off his face, acting as if it never happened. He looks so different from when I met him. He switches back when he realized I wasn't going to let him back up. He starts screaming at the top of his lungs, "You're cheating!"

We broke up six years ago. Does he really believe we're still together?

"That's not my baby!" he shouts in broken English. He switches in and out right before my eyes. Just at that moment, blue and whites come by. A police officer looked at my eyes. Say no more. Her partner frisked him. He found drugs and a kitchen knife on him. Surely, he won't get out now, report after report with over ten domestic violence arrests alone. This guy is not a gangsta. He's a wacko. In Tony Montana's words.

"No wife, no kids."

At court, he pulls on my ribs, practically fracturing them. I scream, "Yo!" to the C.O. He says, "We're here for the magistrate, call 911." I said, "Can you call?" "I'm busy fighting for my life." I thought no phones were allowed in the courthouse anyway.

After that, two detectives come to my house, telling me he's a fugitive and wanted from three other states. A week later, the bounty hunters said they were looking for him. His lawyer calls me and tells me, "He would've faced less time doing murder charges then what I'm charging him with." I replied, "He's charging himself because he did those crimes, not me." I took it more as a threat. That night my phone rang; he was calling me from jail. I thought they record those things. He's saying he is going to hurt me.

Now, he's rotting in jail and that's all. I'm safe. I start to relax. I stop watching over my shoulder. I've got to get out before he's released.

The nightmares are so vivid.

"I see ghosts when I sleep, I had to wake up just to know I was sleep."

My boy told me at the first sight of sunrise, pray when God just wakes, "Please cast him out."

I never saw him again.

Chapter 12

Just as one problem ends, another begins: Starvation. I knew it well as a child, but I never thought that problem would return. Malnutrition is a real, physical thing. I'm weak and tired, but on a mission. I know how to work, but my legs feel like bricks. It's hard to make decisions when you're hungry.

The sun's burning on my face and I think of my ancestors. I'm walking to and from work, and everything looks like biscuits and chicken. Restaurants are open, but I can't go in. Everything's closed when you got no money. Stay alive.

It takes me a while to get back on my feet. Between doctor appointments, teacher conferences, preparing breakfast, lunch, dinner, and snacks. Doing hair, homework, laundry, and baths. Running errands, giving advice, and even doing a project due in the morning. Emergencies pop up at any time, from broken bones to vaccinations. A 72-hour eviction notice on the door, lights cut off, not to mention the cable bill on top. Kids need their cable. In the hood, we don't have lenders or credit cards. We have no hedgehog funds. Hey, it's hard to get food stamps.

I look up at the sky. It's impossible to see stars in NYC, but I see what I think is a shooting star. Then I see another. I now hear my fallen family and friends' voices. Life in the hood is hard but you can make it.

There he is, the chicken. Another one. I try to grab him; he's snotty and runs away just like a New Yorker. It makes me laugh.

There's hope and innocence everywhere: a new baby, the elderly showing me love. I learned to respect life in all forms. Some people got lost for blood money, and some people got lost for no reason at all. My body is covered in Rest in Peace tattoos. Memories in the corner of my mind. I miss my people. I wonder what they could have been.

I visit the block again and see Gee. He hugs me and tells me how he wants out. I said, "Just go, who's gonna stop you?" A few weeks later, I found out the feds took him. He got Life.

I never understood why everyone always comes back, but now I do. My professor was right then: there is no way out. Maybe it's the tree cracklings from the deer, the thought of a bear, or perhaps Freddy. It's not the usual sounds of baby cries, people fighting, dogs barking, sirens, gunshots, and helicopters. My slang, my walk, my talk. The place I always come back to.

My block.